The Ultimate Guide to

Social Media Marketing

How to Use Social Media to Grow Your Business in

Snapchat, Instagram, Facebook, Twitter and

YouTube

MICHAEL MEDIA

Michael Media

Table of Contents

INTRODUCTION 8

WHY SOCIAL MEDIA MARKETING WORKS 8

WHO SHOULD BE USING SOCIAL MEDIA MARKETING? 10

CREATING YOUR SOCIAL MEDIA PRESENCE 11

CHAPTER 1: LINKEDIN 16

SETTING UP YOUR LINKEDIN COMPANY PAGE 16

THE PERFECT STRATEGY 19

ADVERTISING ON LINKEDIN 21

IS YOUR MARKETING STRATEGY WORKING? 23

CHAPTER 2: YOUTUBE 24

USING YOUTUBE FOR BUSINESS 24

CREATING CONTENT TO PROMOTE YOUR BUSINESS 24

QUALITIES OF A GOOD VIDEO 26

SEARCH AND RECOMMENDATION ALGORITHMS 29

CREATING A VIDEO TITLE 30

GROWING YOUR CHANNEL 31

CHAPTER 3: INSTAGRAM 32

STEPS IN SETTING UP INSTAGRAM FOR BUSINESS 33

IMPORTANCE OF AN INSTAGRAM BUSINESS ACCOUNT 37

BUILDING VALUE FOR YOUR INSTAGRAM BUSINESS ACCOUNT 38

CHAPTER 4: SNAPCHAT 40

IS YOUR BRAND COMPATIBLE WITH SNAPCHAT? 41

MEASURE THE RETURN ON INVESTMENT 42

PICK YOUR AUDIENCE 43

HOW DOES SNAPCHAT CONTRAST AND VARIOUS SOCIAL MEDIA STRATEGIES? 43

CRUSADING WITH SNAPCHAT...44

TRY NOT TO GET LAZY 45

CHAPTER 5: TIKTOK **48**

TIKTOK FOR BUSINESS...48

TIPS TO OPTIMIZE YOUR ACCOUNT 49

EXPLORING TIKTOK...50

GET IN FRONT OF THE CAMERA 52

SO HOW ARE BIG COMPANIES TAKING ADVANTAGE OF TIKTOK'S GROWING
VIRALITY?..53

CHAPTER 6: BLOGGING **56**

HOW TO CREATE A BUSINESS BLOG? 56

CREATE MEANS FOR READERS TO SUBSCRIBE..56

ALLOW YOUR BLOG TO BE ON THE SAME DOMAIN AS YOUR WEBSITE 57

CREATE BUSINESS BOOSTING CONTENTS..57

CREATE ENOUGH CONTENTS FOR YOUR BUSINESS BLOG 57

ENSURE THE SHARE BUTTONS ARE PRESENT 57

ENSURE THAT THE BLOG LOADS FASTER..58

WHAT TO KEEP IN MIND WHILE RUNNING A BUSINESS BLOG? 58

CHAPTER 7: BRAND PERSONA OF YOUR BUSINESS **60**

WHO ARE YOU AND WHY ARE YOU DIFFERENT? 61

IDENTIFYING YOUR VOICE 65

CHAPTER 8: CREATING AN ONLINE PRESENCE **68**

BECOMING A BLOGGER...69

MAILING LISTS 70

SOCIAL MEDIA..72

VIDEO STREAMING..75

CHAPTER 9: SOCIAL MEDIA TOOLS **78**

CHOOSING THE BEST SOCIAL MEDIA PLATFORM FOR YOUR JOB IN MARKETING
....78

GOOGLE ANALYTICS 79

ANALYTICS FROM THE INTERNET 79

PERFORMANCE OF WEBSITES...80

ANALYTICS FOR MARKET..80

BIT.LY...81

BUFFER 82

DOSHARE 82

FEEDLY 83

MAILCHIMP..84

**CHAPTER 10: TIPS AND SUGGESTIONS FOR YOUR BUSINESS TO BE
MORE ONLINE** **86**

TWEETING CUSTOMER SERVICE...86

GETTING TO KNOW YOUR BRAND..87

CREATING A STORY ABOUT YOUR BRAND 87

ESTABLISHING BRAND HEROES 87

ENGAGING YOUR CUSTOMERS...88

PUTTING A SPOTLIGHT ON THEM...88

CREATING VALUE-ADDED CONTENT 88

EXPLORING DIGITAL MEDIA..89

THE POWER OF INFLUENCERS..89

10 RULES FOR USING SOCIAL MEDIA TO GROW YOUR COMPANY........................89

CONCLUSION **94**

Michael Media

Introduction

Social media marketing is possibly one of the most well-known forms of digital marketing in recent years. It may also be one of the most powerful strategies to add to your digital marketing efforts, depending on how strong your plan is and how well you execute it. Regardless of what form of company you are running for your digital marketing platform, social media is a tool that you need to be using if you are going to generate any level of success going forward into 2021. In this portion, we will discuss why social media marketing is an essential tool in 2021 and how you can leverage it and how it can be combined with other marketing tools to create a complete digital marketing strategy.

Why Social Media Marketing Works

You may have noticed that we have been stressing one of the most important digital marketing elements in 2021: *personal connection*. These days, people are tired of service that is automated to the point that it is no longer personal or customizable. They want to receive personalized service, suited exactly to their needs, and capable of helping them feel like they are part of something bigger and more important. They want to see the "face" behind the business they are dealing with, and they want to feel like they have some form of connection with the person they are doing business with. That is unless you have billions of dollars to pour into advertising and state-of-the-art automation services as Amazon, Walmart, or other mega giants do for their online services.

As a beginner, however, you will need to create a face for your company that people can identify, get to know, and feel comfortable doing business with. This is where social media comes into play. Social media is a tool that was designed to help people keep in touch. Originally, it was a great opportunity for family members and long-lost friends to reconnect and keep up with each other's lives through social sharing. However, it has become an incredibly powerful marketing tool that people can take advantage of, too, especially because it lets smaller businesses create a name, profile, and personality for themselves online.

When you incorporate social media into your digital marketing strategy, you allow yourself to create business pages for your company, which allows you to share updates with your audience. In a sense, you allow yourself to really engage with your audience in a way that feels like you are friends, rather than in a way that feels like you are just another business trying to earn their money. For this reason, social media is one of the most powerful tools for building and maintaining relationships with your followers and customers.

Beyond helping you create a presence that establishes a social connection with your followers, social media has become one of the most popular places for consumers to find new businesses to shop through. These days, platforms like Facebook, Instagram, Twitter, YouTube, Pinterest, and even LinkedIn are all platforms where people are searching for new businesses to shop through. Getting on these platforms and establishing a presence for yourself means that when people begin to look for someone to shop through on these social sharing sites, they come across your profile. If you did not have a profile, they would be less likely to find you.

Social media platforms are becoming a more and more popular platform for people to search for new businesses because social media sites also come with word-of-mouth marketing built right in. When a consumer lands on a new profile, they can judge just by scrolling whether or not the company is relevant and the quality of services they offer. Companies that have great engagement with their followers and which seem to have positive relationships with their customers are ones that people will automatically begin to trust, regardless of whether or not they have heard of the company before. Just having a strong social media presence can set the tone for inbound marketing to take place which, as you will learn about, is one great strategy for really leveraging social media marketing.

Who Should Be Using Social Media Marketing?

Given the popularity and power of social media marketing, everyone who intends to make any money online should engage with this marketing strategy. If you want to earn money online, creating a social media presence to make money is a great opportunity. Even if you plan on doing most of your marketing through paid advertisements, establishing a presence, and putting up a few organic (non-paid) posts to nurture that presence is a great opportunity to build your business. For most platforms, if you do not have an account, you cannot engage in native marketing, one of the most powerful paid marketing strategies that digital marketers can use going into 2021. So, in short, if you are running a business online or plan on making any level of money online, you need to establish some form of presence on social media to help leverage you into higher levels of success with your business.

Creating Your Social Media Presence

The first step in generating a social media marketing strategy is to create your social media presence. For many people, creating a basic presence is all they will ever need to do. They use this to leverage their growth elsewhere on the internet. In essence, the social media presence is exclusively designed to help identify new target clients and lead them elsewhere to engage with the business either in person or on their website. For others, their social media presence is their primary source for finding new clients, as well as nurturing those relationships and creating sales. Which method you choose will depend on where your primary sales are being made, and how. Suppose your primary strategy will be selling products online on a platform like Amazon, Etsy, Shopify, or Big Cartel. In that case, you might favor paid advertisements over organic marketing, and so your presence may be more basic. If, however, your primary strategy will be affiliate marketing or running your own business on your website, you are likely going to need a stronger social media presence to help funnel more people through your sales process.

Creating any level of presence on social media all works in the same way; the only difference is how much you will be posting on your platform. If you only need a basic presence, a few posts per month will be plenty to help you succeed with your business strategy on social media. If you need a bigger presence, you will want to post a few times per week, or even a couple of times per day, depending on what type of presence you need to establish for success in your digital marketing strategy.

You can start creating your presence by identifying what platforms your audience hangs out on the most and then create a profile on these platforms. When you create your profiles, make sure that you are creating them for your business and not for yourself. This means that you need to use your business name, a username relevant to your business, and images that are all relevant to your business so that it represents your brand rather than yourself. If you are your brand, pick certain aspects of yourself to highlight your feed and leave the rest behind. For example, if you are going to become a fashion influencer and leverage digital marketing to earn an income, center your profile around fashion and your passion for design, and leave your love for mechanics out of it. This way, you create a profile that is relevant to what your audience wants to be seeing. Later on, when you are more established, it may make sense to begin incorporating smaller amounts of other areas of your life into your presence if you are an influencer. This gives you a more personal and "real" element. By sharing small segments of other parts of your life, you show that you are a dynamic person interested in many things, not just the one you market for, which can improve your relationship with your followers by increasing your relatability. If you are a specific brand and not an influencer, though, always keep your posting entirely focused on exactly what your brand represents, and nothing more.

These days, there are countless blogs, articles, and books out there telling you about how you can design a branded profile for your social media platforms. That being said, many of them still have a cold, corporate marketing strategy involved that results in you creating a presence that is very isolated from your audience. Suppose you follow many of the strategies that worked in recent years. In that case, you may end up building a profile that has an invisible "wall" between you and your audience, making it more challenging for them to connect and resonate with you. You need to make sure that you are openly cultivating your presence and encourages engagement right from the start so that people feel comfortable connecting with you and doing business with you.

The best way to create this personalized, friendly experience through your platforms is to look at every single element as an opportunity to create a *personal* connection with your audience e.g. whenever you use images that involve faces and language that connects you with your audience. Another example is instead of saying, "I am an artist looking to share my art," you could say, "I am an artist looking to share my passions with you." This form of connection-based language helps people instantly feel that the ice has been broken the minute they land on your profile, making it easier for them to engage with the content that you have made available for them to see. When you create this type of personal connection through your language and images, people instantly feel like they are your friend and are more likely to trust in you and all that you have to share with them.

When you first create your presence on social media, in addition to creating a profile, you should also upload at least 3-6 posts right away, or within the first hour or two of creating your profile. This way, whenever someone finds your page, they instantly find some content for them to look at as well, making your profile more worthy of staying on for a while than a bare page. This will also help your early page visitors decide if they want to follow you or not, which will build the momentum of new followers finding and engaging with your page online.

CHAPTER 1:

LinkedIn

With more than 562 million members from all over the world, LinkedIn is the largest and most popular professional network. If you want to develop your relationships and grow your network, it is an absolute must for your company to be involved on LinkedIn. It is, after all, the lead generation's largest social network.

LinkedIn, being a website that links companies and experts, requires a unique marketing strategy, of course. The law here is the word of mouth. It's not about whom you know, but whom, through the people you know, you can connect with. But it won't turn out to be a successful marketing campaign to sell your brand through your obsolete personal page. Read on to see how your winning marketing strategy can be developed (and implemented) to get you to the top on LinkedIn.

Setting Up Your LinkedIn Company Page

You need a full-blown business profile for marketing your brand on LinkedIn. The business page is a professional way to let members of LinkedIn know about your name, your products, your organization, and the job opportunities provided by your company.

Although the business websites were mainly used as HR landing pages, this website now offers a great opportunity to raise awareness of the brand and market your services to potential clients.

You need an active personal profile on LinkedIn first to set up a company website. If you have one, just follow the next steps to build your company's website.

1. Add your company

Go to https:/business.linkedin.com/marketing/LinkedIn accounts and click 'Edit Your Account'. Type your company name and create a URL to help people find your website. Note that later you won't be able to change the URL, so make sure you choose wisely. Then check the checkbox to check that you are the company's official representative and click' Launch Account.'

The shell will be created automatically. Only press the 'Get Started' button to start creating your website.

2. Add your image

Import your logo (recommended 300x 300 pixels) as your profile image and add a cover image (preferably 1536x 768 px) to give an insight into what your business is about. Keep in mind that logos businesses have more traffic, so don't be tempted to miss this phase.

3. Create Your Description

LinkedIn allows you to use 2,000 characters for your description, but be aware that it is the first 156 words that are displayed on Google in the preview of your company page, so make sure you write an excellent start.

You have 20 specialties to add. Think of them as keywords advertisements that can help people discover their business on LinkedIn, so be sure to reflect the business ' power and knowledge here.

4. Company details

Here you enter the location of your company, the URL of your website, your industry, the size and form of your product, as well as other important details identifying your company.

5. Publish the page

Tap ' Publish' to go online. It is best to see what the business page looks like when other people press on it before you start. Tap ' Member Window' to try it out. If the look of your page is not satisfied, go to' Manage Page' and make some modifications.

6. Page Administrators

If you're not planning to run your LinkedIn Company page alone, you'll need to select the people you can administer the page.

Tap on the 'Me' button at the top of your screen to add more staff. Go to 'Manage', and then select your Company Page. There, pick the 'Admin Tools' option for 'Web Admins'. Enter the name of the users you want to view the list.

Note: To pick them as admins, you must already be linked to these individuals on LinkedIn.

The Perfect Strategy

Only having a business website doesn't mean you're going to get the right connections. You also need to have a good marketing plan for LinkedIn, just like any other site. Here's what you can do to improve your chances of success:

- Create a Showcase Page

Showcase pages are the perfect way to display a particular part of your company you're most proud of. This is a great opportunity to put your best product in the spotlight and attract potential customers.

The view pages act as some kind of subdomains for your business website. Having one can really make a difference because members on LinkedIn can also visit them individually if they are specifically interested in a particular product or service. You can have pages up to view.

Tap the' Me ' button to build one, then pick your Company Page under' Manage.' Then go to' Admin Tools'—' Create a page for a showcase.'

- Have Your Employees Connected

Your employees are your biggest advocates on LinkedIn. Having them as followers means you have access to their networks and connections, which can increase your reach significantly and bring more traffic to your company page. Encourage your employees to be connected to your company page to raise awareness of the brand.

- Keep Followers Informed

The easiest way to boost your market is to be happy with the one you have. Make sure you write valuable content on your business on a regular basis, such as blogs, blog posts, or other updates. Even, if you can conceive of a worthwhile external post for your fans, do not hesitate to publish it as well.

- Choose LinkedIn Groups

LinkedIn Groups provide you with a perfect way to connect with people in your immediate circle from your profession. Active in a LinkedIn Community and engaged in conversations will lead to more visits to your site.

Would you like to find a group that suits your goal? With the 'Group Discover' option, you can check out some suggestions for LinkedIn, or just use the search bar if you know what you're looking for.

- Go Global

If you have clients in some countries where English is not the official language, then you may want to consider adding a summary in other languages of your product. Don't worry, for that reason you don't have to find a translator. LinkedIn offers multi-language tools for you to take care of this.

- Publish at the Right Times

Like the plans for your other sites, you also need to schedule your LinkedIn posting. Data from LinkedIn says the best time to post material on LinkedIn is in the morning and after business hours. This is when people are most involved, so you may want to take advantage of this knowledge and then plan your message.

Advertising on LinkedIn

If you want to direct your message to other practitioners, whether CEOs or influencers, you should definitely take advantage of ads on LinkedIn. You will start with the next steps after you decide what you want to promote and who is your target audience.

- Your 'Campaign Manager' Account

First of all, you need to have a' Campaign Manager ' account to take care of here https:/www.linkedin.com/ad-beta/login. This is a tool that gives you the easiest way to manage and automate your advertising. However, this app provides some useful tools to show the output of your ads, so it's an added bonus.

- Choose the Type of Your Ad

Next, the type of ad you want to advertise must be selected. Three options are available:

➢ Sponsored InMail
➢ Sponsored content
➢ Text Ad

With all three forms, you can also build your advertisement to ensure maximum coverage.

Once you choose the ad form, enter your campaign name, select the language of your target audience, and select the call-to-action feature, which is only available for the Sponsored-Content advertisements.

- Create the Ad

The best thing about the Campaign Manager is to guide you through the production steps, giving advice and guidance along the way. Follow the steps choosing the most appropriate choices for your target.

- Target the Ad

Make sure your ad is aimed at the right people at this point. You may state such requirements such as location, names of classes, company names, degree, job title, class, age, years of experience, qualifications, etc. Make sure that you save your qualifications so that the next time you want to advertise on LinkedIn you can speed things up.

- Set the Budget and Schedule

There are three options you can pay for ads:

1. Cost per click (CPC)
2. Cost per impression (CPM)–for user display messages
3. Cost per send–for supported InMail advertising (here you only pay for receiving messages)

For the CPM and CPS alternative, you are allowed to set a maximum daily budget you are willing to spend and a bid price. Just plan the beginning and end date and time for the ad after that, and you're done.

Is Your Marketing Strategy Working?

When you take your stats from another social media platform, the real picture of your LinkedIn success is probably missing. Checking out the built-in analytics tool on LinkedIn is the best way to check whether your marketing strategy works.

Go to the top of your screen toolbar fount and press the' Analytics' tab. You can see that there are three options available:

- *Visitors*-This is where data is stored on the people visiting your website. Here you can see a general overview of page views, user stats, you can separate data from a certain time and date, see data from different sites on your site, and see detailed information about users visiting your page (job feature, venue, sector, etc.)
- *Feedback*–here you can find information about the content you post. Such indicators of communication include views, downloads, shares, comments, taps, etc.
- *Followers*–You can analyze your list of supporters in more depth in the' Followers' tab.

CHAPTER 2:

YouTube

Using YouTube for Business

YouTube is a much different platform in terms of social media. While most other platforms are designed to highlight the interaction between people, YouTube is really about content delivery. At its core, people interact with YouTube, not for the community options that are available, but rather for the purpose of accessing and consuming the content that they are interested in.

YouTube offers businesses two options when it comes to social media marketing. The first option is to become a content creator, working to create video content that is useful for your customer base. The second option is creating and running paid advertisements on YouTube itself, allowing you to get your message in front of relevant customers.

Creating Content to Promote Your Business

You may be wondering if the process of creating videos for YouTube is worth it for your business. After all, you most likely aren't planning on embarking on a professional YouTube career, working to get millions of viewers per day. Doing so is an exhausting effort and truthfully, is an entire business in itself.

Yet, while you may not be interested in the amount of work required to create a YouTube career, it's important to note that by creating your own content, you can greatly promote your own business.

When customers begin researching your products and services, they are most likely going to be looking for hard evidence that the product will help them solve their problems. By having a central location, such as a YouTube channel, where prospective customers can visit and watch your products in action, you'll be increasing the chances of conversion. On top of that, you can create all sorts of different content that will directly help your customer base, such as tutorials, FAQs, product announcements, etc. Let's take a look at the different types of videos that you can create for your business.

- *Tutorials:*

Customers often struggle with complex products all the time. If the product that you have is complicated or requires construction, then you might want to consider making tutorials for those products. The videos themselves don't need to be terribly flashy or over-produced. Rather, they just need to convey all the necessary, step by step actions required to make the product work.

The value of creating these tutorials is that it will help to generate goodwill from your existing customer base. The fact that you are willing to take time out of your day to create these videos and aid your customers with their problem will reflect well on you. On top of that, a potential customer who is curious about how hard it is to build or use the product will be able to watch and get an answer to their questions

- How-To:

In addition to creating tutorials, you can also work to create how-to guides meant to help customers and followers solve problems that aren't necessarily related to your product but are related to your niche. This is a community service and it has the benefit of helping consumers become aware of your product. You are free to pitch your product or website at the end of the video, but if you focus on solving a customer's real problem first, they will be more open to the message that you have at the end.

- Product Demos/Advertisements:

Seeing a product in action is far better than simply imagining what the product can do. By creating product demos, meant to advertise the features and functions of your product, you will be able to help your customers make a faster purchasing decision.

- Interviews and Behind the Scenes:

On top of creating videos meant to promote products, you can also create videos meant simple to promote your company. Shooting a few behind the scenes videos and some interviews will help give your business a sense of depth.

Qualities of a Good Video

If you've decided that you want to create videos for YouTube, then you're going to need to put in the necessary time and energy to make it look and sound good. This can be a bit of work, especially if you're just starting out in the video creation process. However, the good news is that the minimums to making a good video aren't fairly stringent, and once you learn the few underlying principles of good video quality, you can replicate it fairly quickly. Let's take a look at a few different qualities that you'll need to focus on when creating videos.

- Audio and Visual Quality:

In general, you don't need to have extremely expensive filmmaking equipment, especially if you aren't going to be doing anything fancy. Usually, an iPhone can record most things well enough and if you want to upgrade, there are plenty of good cameras that you can get for under $500. As long as you keep the camera stable and focused, you shouldn't have too much trouble operating the camera.

However, while the video quality is important, you must also make sure not to neglect audio quality. Most equipment used to capture video doesn't do that great of a job capturing audio, so you'll need to make sure that you invest some money in a separate microphone, especially if there's going to be extensively talking in the video. A good recommendation for a stand-alone mic with plenty of functionality would be the Blue Yeti. It works well, captures great audio, and doesn't require anything other than a laptop for recording

- *Lighting:*

Another factor to consider is lighting. If you're going to be showing products off, then you're going to need to make sure that you have a good lighting set. Most kits are fairly inexpensive and will include all of the necessary components to taking great videos that are both clean and crisp.

- *Script:*

Unless the event that you are recording is a live one or meant to be behind the scenes, then you're going to want to put any effort into creating the script for your video ahead of time. A script, even if it's just a general one, will help your actors to stay focused in the video, stay on topic and most importantly, deliver all of the relevant facts to the viewer.

A good script gets to the point as quickly as possible. Some viewers don't have a lot of patience, especially when it comes to watching a video meant to help them solve a problem. Clicking on a video that promises to help solve a problem, only to find yourself waiting 5 minutes as the video talks about something irrelevant can be frustrating. In some cases, these viewers may even end up exiting the video and going to look for another guide.

If you want to stop this from happening, then start out with the information that the viewer is looking for. Bring this as soon as possible. This will help satisfy their needs and more importantly, encourage them to finish watching the entire video. Then, as the video winds down, you can pitch your website, your products, or whatever else you want to share with them. Remember, provide value first, and once you have earned that connection with the viewer, then talk about what you want to talk about.

Search and Recommendation Algorithms

YouTube is a mix between a content discovery engine and a search engine. YouTube viewers have a recommended feed, that is constantly showing them video recommendations that the algorithms believe are most relevant to the user. On top of that, searching for generic terms will bring up the most relevant videos possible, so that users are able to get the best viewing experience.

There are a few factors that go into the YouTube search algorithms. The first and foremost is viewing time for a video channel. The more hours that a video is watched, the more likely it is to show up on the recommended list or in the search bar. While views are important, a view doesn't hold as much value as viewing time. If ten people click on a video, but only one watches it all the way to the end, YouTube will get an understanding that the video itself isn't very valuable. It will rank the video accordingly and it most likely won't be recommended.

Another way that YouTube ranks videos is by their descriptions. By adding the proper keywords to your descriptions, you will be increasing your chances of YouTube finding your video when someone types in a search. It's important to make sure that your keyword usage is organic and doesn't include heavy strings of random keywords stuffed together. The old SEO practice of keyword stuffing is long dead and most search algorithms actually work to ignore that practice. Instead, just create video descriptions that organically include the proper keywords that are relevant to your niche. On top of that, if you really want to increase the chances of the search engine picking up your videos, you should also include subtitles, which will be indexed by the search engine. Then, it will be keenly aware of all the keywords you are using in your video.

Creating a Video Title

One of the most important aspects of getting people to watch your videos is to make sure that you have an interesting and relevant title. As a rule of thumb, you will want the title to be as self-explanatory as possible. So, if you're posting a video that helps with solving a tech problem, simply title it "How to Solve X." You might want to add a few descriptive words that will help pull the viewer in, such as "Fast Ways to Fix X," or "Ridiculously Simple Fix for X."

These types of descriptors are useful for drawing a consumer in and getting them to click on the video itself. Unless they have specifically set out to watch your video, you're going to have to rely on the title and the thumbnail to convince someone to click on your video. A catchy, straightforward title with good descriptors is a good way to go.

However, you must take care to avoid creating titles that are known as *clickbait*. These titles often having shocking or extremely interesting ideas presented to the viewers, but when you click on them and actually watch the video, the title is somewhat exaggerated or even irrelevant.

Be honest with your titles. It may be tempting to exaggerate or present false information in order to get people to click on your video, but they won't stick around for the whole thing. Viewing time is regarded as more important than simple clicks, so don't take the risk.

Growing Your Channel

Once you've created your YouTube channel, you'll want to increase the number of subscribers that you have. However, it is important to realize that unless you are seriously focusing on growing your channel, subscriber amount isn't the most important thing in the world. When it comes to things like product demos or tutorials, the numbers of views will most likely not climb terribly high at first, however, these views themselves are valuable because they represent a customer who is looking to you for assistance with your products.

What you want to focus on is creating ways for your consumers to be able to access your videos easily. The easier it is for potential consumers and your current customer base to locate and enjoy your videos, the better chance your channel has of growing.

CHAPTER 3:

Instagram

T o realize the full potential of Instagram for your business, the first step, of course, is to set up a Business Instagram account, which is pretty different from the normal personalized accounts and offers additional features essential for your business marketing needs. With an increasing number of users daily, through your Instagram business accounts, you can share and attract millions of potential customers through graphically rich photos and videos portraying inspiring stories about your brand or business and why they should choose your business or brand over the rest in the global market.

Also, before setting up an Instagram account, it's important to have a strategy just like in your business plan. Ask yourself, what is the aim of setting up the Instagram business account? Possibly it could be to find new customers, expand the market for your products globally, promote a specific product to increase sales, share your company's culture that may be deemed satisfying to customers, or even to discover and learn the latest trends in the industry that you can implement in your business. Whatever your aim, always have a clear strategy like a blueprint, as it will help you achieve your goal.

Steps in Setting Up Instagram for Business

Instagram works synonymously with Facebook; therefore, you will need to have a business Facebook page setup before opening an Instagram business account and linking it to your Facebook page.

Having a LinkedIn or Twitter account will be advantageous for your business as it will enable you to reach out to other prospective customers who may not be using Instagram or following your business account on Instagram

1. *Download the Instagram app*

Instagram is quite different from other social media platforms such as Facebook and Twitter since posting videos and photos can only be done through the Instagram app. Therefore, you will need to download from the in-app purchases portions in the Play Store for Android devices and the App Store for iOS devices. The file size is about 2.0 MB and you should not worry about the space on your device.

2. *Using an Email Address to Create your Account*

You should have an email address for your business prior to opening an Instagram account for your business. It is advisable to create an account based on the profile on your Facebook page or other social media account including Twitter and LinkedIn, as it will go a long way in ensuring prospective customers identify your business easily on all these social media platforms. Also, using a personal or work email address when setting up your business account will ensure that your contacts easily find you using the **Find Friends** tab.

3. *Choose a Username*

The next step will be to choose a username coupled with a password for security purposes. Always ensure that when choosing a username, it should be the company's name or a close variation. Also, if you are a real estate agent, salesperson, insurance agent, or any agent, you should choose a username that closely ties with your personal name, location, or business and differentiates your business account from your personal account. For instance, in the case of a real estate agent, Micheal Williams-NYC-realtor, or Micheal Williams-LA-ins for the case of an insurance agent. Don't worry if you can't come up with a suitable name since Instagram can automatically generate a username based on the keyed profile name.

4. *Uploading a Profile Photo*

Your profile photo says a lot about your business or profession; therefore, it is important to pick the right profile photo. The profile photo should be your business logo or an easily recognizable sign associated with your brand. In the case of your business offering professional services, upload your professional headshot image donning professional attire, for example, a white coat in the case of medical professionals or a helmet and reflector jackets in the case of real estate agents or engineers. To upload a profile photo, tap the **Add a photo** tab where you will be given several upload options including an option to upload a profile photo from Facebook or Twitter. You can upload your profile photo from other social media accounts if they are your business account. After uploading a profile photo, save your info by clicking

Done located in the top right corner to eliminate the need for password inputs while logging in to your account and to accelerate future logins.

5. *Complete your Profile*

After uploading your profile photo, complete your profile by clicking on the **Edit Your Profile** button and filling the required fields, which are a name, username, website, bio, email, contact info, and gender. The website field is significant for your business as it is the only portion where your account visitors are automatically directed to your website after clicking on the URL. A URL posted in the comment portion of a post is void and users may not be able to access your website through the URL posted. The biofield is also limited to a few characters, therefore you must be brief in explaining the type of business, services or products offered, location, and why people should choose your brand over the rest.

6. *Switch to Instagram for Business.*

This is the most important step in setting up an Instagram business account. It distinguishes a personalized account from a business account. It allows you to access Instagram for business tools, perfect for any business. On the **Edit Profile** page, find and tap on the **Try Instagram Business Tools** button to automatically be directed to **Settings** in the **Switch to business account** tab. After clicking on the button, you will be required to upload information about your business including opening hours, phone number, and your business address. With an Instagram business account, you can access insights about your posts, stories, and even your account followers.

7. Link your Business Instagram Account to your Business Facebook page.

We already stated the need to have a Facebook business page to reach out to prospective customers who may not be on Instagram. Instagram will automatically ask you to link your Facebook page to the created account. A Facebook business page is also important for you to use Instagram for Business tools.

8. Find Facebook friends & contacts.

After setting up an account and linking it to your business Facebook page, Instagram will automatically recommend people to follow based on your Facebook page followers or contact information. You can skip this platform based on the strategy or idea of setting up an Instagram business page. For instance, maybe you would need a completely new market for your product or may not prefer your contacts following your Instagram business page. In later topics, we will discuss building value for your business by gaining followers and monetizing them.

9. Start Posting

Start posting content deemed appropriate for your business field using relevant captions and hashtags. Also, after posting, follow similar accounts who have tagged their contents using the same hashtag. Through hashtags, millions of photos are arranged in one virtual location like a database, thereby enabling users to locate accounts easily, thus your business account can easily be located by prospective customers, adding value to business marketing needs. Additionally, use popular hashtags such as #happy, #love, #tbt as they are used by millions of users thereby exposing your business for easy access by prospective customers. Use a specific hashtag, for instance, #realestate or #property if you are targeting a forte of customers.

Importance of an Instagram Business Account

- You can add information relating to your company such as location, business hours, and phone number, therefore it is convenient for your customers.

- With the swipe-up feature in the story timeline, you insert a link to redirect your followers to anywhere appropriate, be it your web page or your YouTube channel, increasing your sales conversion potential. This tool can be your oyster specifically if you have a business profile with over 10k followers.

- With an Instagram business account, you can legitimize your business creating an impression of legality in prospective customers. Highlighting your brand profile using an Instagram business account has turned out to be the ideal way of legitimizing your business, especially through the blue verification checkmark. This, in turn, attracts numerous customers who would want to buy products or services from legitimate businesses as they are assured of the quality of the product or service being advertised.

- An Instagram business account enables you to utilize Instagram's native shopping function. This feature enables businesses with an Instagram business account to grow their brand by acquiring new customers who drive sales in very indirect ways. Most people on Instagram discover a product but may not purchase right there and then but would come back to purchase the product after getting some cash. With this tool, users can obtain a lot more information about the product thereby assisting them in deciding to buy a product.

Building Value for your Instagram Business Account

The essence of creating an Instagram business account is to market your brand globally by uploading videos and photos of your brand. Therefore, it is important to gain followers who may be possible customers thereby building value for your business. Gaining followers on Instagram is not as difficult as on other social media platforms such as Facebook and Twitter since Instagram recommends who to follow based on your contact information or Facebook business page once you are done setting up your account. Once you follow users, they will follow you back if your brand is relevant to their needs or demands. Additionally, Instagram notifies your Facebook contacts on Instagram once you set up an account, therefore, it can help drive followers, but you should have other strategies of gaining followers as we are going to discuss below. With over ten thousand followers, you can monetize your Instagram account using several approaches as we will discuss later. First, lets us look at strategies you can use for your Instagram business account to gain over ten thousand followers.

- Use the right hashtags

As mentioned earlier, hashtagging your photos and videos is vital in ensuring you expand your audience by growing your following, as it makes it straightforward for users to locate and view your photos or videos after searching for specific names or hashtags. By using the right hashtags to tag your content, it's more likely that your account or product is easily discoverable by new users.

Finding the most relevant hashtag to tag your content can be hectic. Therefore you can use online tools such as Websta or IconoSuare. These tools enable you to find related and popular hashtags for your brand. They indicate the number of times a hashtag has been used. Note that Instagram allows a maximum of 30 hashtags per post, therefore, you have a wide category of hashtags to choose from. Additionally, you can steal hashtags from similar accounts or your competitors. Still, it is not advisable as you would want to create a relatable group of hashtags specific to your account. There are several ways to create hashtags for your brand such as Brand keyword Hashtags – #mybrandname, #fashion, #menswear. Product category hashtags – #socks, #happysocks, #sockswagg. Specific location hashtags – #LA, #LAfashion, #LAtrends, and so much more.

CHAPTER 4:

Snapchat

T he hours of Facebook and Twitter as the dominating web-based life powers are done. Today, there are a couple of online life arranges, each with novel claims to fame and examples. While it may have all the earmarks of being prudent from the outset to create followings on every other option, this isn't down to earth.

You'll see that your prime leads contribute most of their vitality in explicit stages and no time on others. Find your customers and go where they contribute their vitality for ground-breaking on the web life publicizing. Among the new online life platform options, one of the snappiest creating is Snapchat, so promoters subsequently acknowledge they should take their piece of that potentially advantageous pie.

Snap Inc. is Snapchat's parent association and holds a current market valuation of around $25 billion. While working on benefitting by this may seem, by all accounts, to be a simple choice, this web-based life platform isn't perfect for each brand.

Snapchat reports forceful customer duty stood out from other web-based life stages. Many individuals check online life applications reliably, at times a couple of times every day. Customers check Snapchat on numerous occasions each day all things considered, and over 2.5 billion snaps make an excursion through the framework to more than 150 million customers reliably.

To be sure, over 45% of all of the 18-to 55-year-olds in the United States use Snapchat. If you have to exploit this conceivably huge accomplishment, you ought to carefully consider how to utilize Snapchat reasonably for your picture.

Is Your Brand Compatible with Snapchat?

Snapchat empowers customers to send photos and brief chronicles to their friends and lovers on the application. Customers can change their photos with emoji images, substance, and drawing instruments. Some influencers on Snapchat support their get-together of individuals people to attract with them by simply releasing Snaps briefly.

Snaps are similarly transient – when a customer sees a Snap picture or video, they simply have several minutes with it before it's gone until the cows come home. Customers can take screen catches of Snaps, yet the window for doing as such is obliged.

Dependent upon the sort of business you run, this could be a weighty kind of duty for your get-together of individuals. Regardless, Snapchat customers float on the younger side, so aside from on the off chance that you can get this measurement's energy, it may not merit your time. Sponsors defy goliath strain to drive their brands' web-based life duty with their gatherings of spectators. It's basic not to lounge around inactively where your undertakings exhibit useless.

Measure the Return on Investment

Each exhibiting endeavor should try a positive pace of return (ROI). Put just, on the off chance that you're not getting more than what you put assets into a campaign strategy, that framework isn't functional and, in all probability, won't remain appropriate for long. Snapchat is expensive for marketing experts because of the potential for high duty levels.

Most standard publicizing models for Snapchat use a cost for each impression show. Fundamentally, you pay for each time customers see your substance. Sadly, for publicists enthused about Snapchat, the platform isn't all around arranged for nearly nothing or creating associations.

The base spends for publicizing on Snapchat is a dazzling $40,000. Exceptional advancement models that chip away to a detriment for each swipe show are in like manner exorbitant. But on the off chance that you have the liquidity to contribute that much for a perhaps uncertain outcome, the base buy-in is a strong obstacle.

You could tailor your Snapchat advancing using a wonderful geo-filter for the most astute outcomes. As the name proposes, a geo-filter centers around your substance to an unequivocal territory. This can be reasonable for neighborhood associations who need to contact more people in their overall region. Snapchat will consider the range of the domain you have to target and the assessed action volume in the midst of an offered period to choose the cost.

Pick Your Audience

For the most part, Snapchat just fills in as a publicizing platform for business-to-customer affiliations. If you work in a business-to-business task, you more likely than not won't find enough master closeness on Snapchat to legitimize investing assets into displaying energy. Snapchat is a quick line to the end customer. If you have to create leads directly from your purchaser base, you may find them on Snapchat.

In like manner consider what kind of product and undertakings your association offers. Do your ideal customer types slant toward the more energetic side? Over 70% of Snapchat customers are younger than 34, so you probably won't see positive results if you consider a more settled market. In case your customers are young and recognize intuitive media content, think about ways to deal with sending them productive substance in photos or videos.

If you can consider a couple of expected results, it may be a perfect chance to start Snapchatting. Over 90% of fights that use Snapchat report bargains that expand, advancing on the platform.

How Does Snapchat contrast and Various Social Media Strategies?

A champion among different contraptions for promoters on Snapchat is the ability to move associations for your group. These associations meet up with customers in an easy-to-investigate manner. Customers simply swipe up to see the substance. Snapchat announced that its swipe-up percentage attains on different occasions further positive results than ordinary explore rates on other advancing channels.

Using Snapchat associations, you can send your gathering of spectator's instructive articles, email select ins, video content, requesting to present your picture's applications, associations with your website and other online long-range interpersonal communication profiles, and essentially more.

If customers are busy with your picture, they'll likely put aside the chance to swipe up through your associations and see what you bring to the table. In case you tailor your Snapchat fight to getting the thought of a more energetic client base, you could possibly extend your picture care.

Crusading with Snapchat

Every business has a fascinating character, and your advancing undertakings on a fun-centered platform like Snapchat should include your human side. Consider the going with when devising better ways to deal with associate with your gathering of spectators:

Talk one-on-one with customers. You may get messages, questions, or responses about your promoting materials from customers. Consider this information significant and attempt to respond to whatever number of customer responsibility could be normal in light of the current situation. Current purchasers love to feel regarded, so demonstrate to them you care by putting aside the chance to address their concerns and respond to their comments solely.

Insider looks. Exhibit your gathering of spectators that proceeds off-camera at your association. If you make stock, consider finishing a walk around your age office to show your customers how you make your things. You could in like manner have merry substance exhibiting your delegates benefiting as much as possible from their time at work and including things that make your association unique.

Work with influencers. Internet organizing influencers have a gigantic reach, so look for Snapchat characters with sizeable followings who make content related to your picture. At the point when you discover a few contenders, approach them with cross-restricted time musings and check whether you can benefit by access to their considerable gatherings of spectators.

Stay in touch. More young people are regularly present at world events. Information adventures quickly, and youths respect associations that can convey something gainful that resonates with the events. Do whatever it takes not to race to post content about the latest examples and events, in any case. Various associations have encountered horrifying payoff their customers over wanton or incapably organized substance releases by means of online systems administration media, so use reasonability while picking what to move.

Try Not to Get Lazy

Another basic conviction to hold up under as a principle need (at any rate until further notice) is that various sponsors despite everything can't comprehend the potential Snapchat has as an exhibiting asset. Your opponent probably won't have considered advancing on Snapchat as a result of the amazing effect Facebook and Twitter have had consistently. Various specialists have removed it as a direct photo-sharing application for youngsters.

Snapchat is certainly more than a period killer for youngsters. Incalculable brands have had accomplishment publicizing on the platform. While the desire to assimilate data and area cost may have all the earmarks of being steep from the outset, analyze the phase to see what potential it has for your picture. If you can tailor a publicizing model to your money related arrangement and goals, you need to make Snapchat-obliging content to start getting the advantages.

Michael Media

CHAPTER 5:

TikTok

TikTok for Business

Recently TikTok announced the name of its new platform and brand called TikTok For Business, which will serve as the home for all of its marketing solutions for brands.

Initially, TikTok For Business will comprise access to TikTok ad arrangements, counting its flagship brand product, Top View, it is the ad that shows when you launch the app for the first time. Other products under this new umbrella include brand acquisitions, videos, hashtag challenges, and effects tailored to brands.

Brand acquisitions are three to five-second ads, typically using a video or image; embedded videos can be up to 60 seconds long and played with the sound on; hashtag challenges allow your brand to engage with your user community, inviting them to create content around a specific hashtag. This also includes Hashtag Plus, which adds a shopping feature to this experience.

On the other hand, the effects tailored to your brand allow you to provide a closer experience when implementing 2D, 3D, or augmented reality formats in your videos. It's a good way to boost hashtag challenges to get better interactions with your audience.

Sponsored video examples can give you helpful strategies related to creative marketing and ideas for experimenting with new platforms. Even if you don't join TikTok, watching these videos can inspire you for your posts on other visual platforms, like Instagram.

Tips to Optimize Your Account

1.   Choose a profile photo that is relevant to the audience

Here is the profile of Gary Vay-Ner-Chuk; one can perceive that he has revised the profile of his account to accommodate the target viewers on the podium (fundamentally a bright). The profile photo is stimulating and pertinent to what most Gen Z'ers are doing nowadays compared to other social media.

Gary Vay-Ner-Chuk

@garyvee

verified account

"If you are a minor corporate, post a photo of you, yourself, as it is easier for users to identify than your business logo and much more human. People want to do business or share fun content with people, not companies. "

2. Make your bio relevant

Here's an opportunity to tell people what you do or, in our case, tell people about your business. If you are looking to promote yourself as a personal brand, you can offer them a URL (like Lisa and Lena, the most popular TikTok user) and send them a message that directly relates to your business-like Apple.

Unlike other platforms, there is not a lot of what you can do with your profile. It is what it produces, which we will see later.

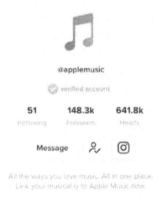

Exploring TikTok

Now that your profile is ready, it is time to enjoy the application is divided into two main channels.

*   For You:

    For You is an algorithmically generated stream of that page's similarities to Instagram's Explore page. This is often the best performing content in your region if you are a new user. If you are a regular user then the algorithm offers you content based on your likes and hashtags.

- Following:

By tapping the Following button at the top of the screen, you can find the content created by the users you choose to follow on TikTok. You will notice to the right of each TikTok video a series of icons. The first will take you to the profile of the user who posted it. Then there is a heart, which is the same as a Facebook like. Following are comments, a right-pointing arrow for input individual TikToks with other podiums, which is an alternative aim for its viral essence. The past icon is a rotating disk with musical notes originating from it. This signifies the excerpt of the song that the user is playing on their TikTok. Click on it to see the track's name and artist, as well as a source from other TikToks that feature it as well. A good example is Joji's "Slow Dancing in The Dark," which has been featured in over 1.2 million videos, as it is combined with the viral microwave challenge I mentioned earlier.

Soak up what's happening on the platform, and get an idea of what you think might work for you by watching other creators as we dive into content creation.

Get In Front Of The Camera

Ready to share your first piece of content?

First, tap the plus sign at the bottom of the screen. The camera will open, showing a red record alike to Snapchat. Beforehand you begin recording, you can augment a song subsequently whatever you choose to share aligns with the beats you choose. If you want to film something as soon as inspiration strikes, you can jump in and start recording without a music track, then add the beats on top.

Similar to Snapchat, TikTok partakes a variety of AR effects that can be utilized in videos, which prepare effects like modifying the color of your eyes or hair. Choose **Effects** on the left side to get access.

There is a Beauty key that faintly removes the dark shadows below the eyes on the right side of the recording screen. Below is the menu of filters, which are numbered. The last feature is its timer, which allows users to film videos without holding the record button or to run some of the challenges that we will discuss.

TikToks may be up to 15 seconds, but then again users can attach several clips collected for up to 60 seconds of the entire recording. You can also upload lengthier videos that have been documented outside of the app.

So How are Big Companies Taking Advantage of TikTok's Growing Virality?

ABC is running the #LikeAnAmericanIdol challenge on TikTok, inviting you to "show your amazing voice." (At the time of writing, there have been 156 million videos with the hashtag.) Google lately ran a comparable challenge movement with the hashtag #HeyGoogleHelp.

The core of what makes TikTok so great is the challenges and the music that goes with them. Here are the three main components that large companies can use as a guide to creating their own challenges.

1. Choose the right path.

When starting out, choose a song with a commercial appeal that ties the lyrics or rhythm of the song to the video's actions. For example, the Yeehaw Challenge is linked to a call to action, which is that the common person transforms from normal to cowboy when the rhythm drops.

2. Make it obvious.

The best challenges and their hashtags make it tremendously clear what it takes to do the task. The microwave challenge is combined with a tune that mimics the same sound that microwaves make, signaling people to complete the action.

3. Make it accessible.

Don't limit people by doing them.

You need something that is not at a low price or items that are not from home. You can give everyone a chance to film their challenge using something they can find at home or your local retail store for a very low price.

Once you've accomplished this, recruit 5-10 of the top-tier influencers on the platform to run the challenge and watch the fire spread. TikTok is made to make great content go viral. All you have to do is have a great company be the fuel to spread it.

CHAPTER 6:

Blogging

How to Create a Business Blog?

Blogs can help as a business strategy for increasing sales and building customers. To create a business blog the steps are:

- Selecting the right blogging niche
- Picking a suitable blogging platform
- Creating your domain name
- Choosing an appropriate hosting plan
- Installing your blogging platform
- Adding functions and changing the look of your blog

For a successful business blog, you must ensure that you do the following:

Create Means for Readers to Subscribe

Using a business blog to help grow marketing, you must provide your audience with a suitable means that can allow them to subscribe to your blog. With the subscription of active readers, your sales increase, and you can convert prospects into customers.

Allow Your Blog to be on the Same Domain as Your Website

Blogging allows you allows you to build the Search Engine Optimization (SEO) value of your business website. Hence, once you add your blog on the same domain as your website, you create an increase in your business website's performance.

Create Business Boosting Contents

Remember, it's a business blog? So, don't just post content but create content that would attract readers to your products. This blog is not only aimed at conversing with readers, but for achieving business goals. Also, people who are willing to purchase your products won't be ready to go through your blog posts if it isn't related to the product and services you offer.

Create Enough Contents for Your Business Blog

With enough content on your blog, you can get more traffic on your blog, which would prove very helpful for your Business. Publish more blogs that can help boost your Business, and help you achieve your marketing goals. Although you should create more blog posts, it is also imperative that you create blog posts with high quality.

Ensure the Share Buttons are Present

A simple way of making your blog successful, you need as many followers as possible. It can also help improve your business. One way of getting traffic on your blog is to enable the share button on your business blog. With this, active readers can share your posts, and more people can start visiting your blog.

Ensure that the Blog Loads Faster

Readers value their time, and they would quickly get pissed off when they notice that your blog has a prolonged loading time. These slowdowns can be a result of adding large-sized visual media (photos and videos). Hence, you must test your blogging site with some remarkable online tools that can help you identify various means of reducing your blog's loading time. An excellent online tool for this purpose is Webpagetest.org.

What to Keep in Mind While Running A Business Blog?

A business blog is not the same as a personal blog, as this blog helps grow your business. Hence, you must take care while running a business blog. Here are some things to take note of for your business blog:

- Always make posts that are related to the products offered by your business
- Let your contents answer the questions of your customers
- Take note of the needs of your audience (you can make use of polls and surveys)
- Write in a conversational tone to engage your readers with your posts

- Make unique newsletters to send your posts to your followers
- Do not be excessively promotional
- Include appropriate visual content
- Portion suitable success stories
- Be fervent around blogging

CHAPTER 7:

Brand Persona of Your Business

As you are building a personal brand, you need to look at it in two layers. The first layer is the technical stuff that you sorted out, which essentially deliberated what the specifics of your business would be. There, you identified what industry you were going to grow into, what niche you would serve, who your audience would be, and what you would be offering to your audience. This part was important for developing the foundation for your business to grow on, as this is how you are going to know what your goals are and whether or not you are achieving them. Now, you need to equip yourself with the tools actually to reach those goals. This is where your brand persona comes in.

Your brand persona is the character or personality of your brand that your audience will interact with. The easiest way to understand this concept is to imagine that your brand's niche, audience, and offerings were the plot of a novel. Your brand persona was the main character. The niche, audience, and offerings would provide the foundation. Still, without the main character, there would be no way to serve the story to the reader. This is what you are doing with your brand persona: developing the main character with whom your target audience can interact, grow to love, and root for. You want your audience to have a person in mind (you) that they can relate to and develop a relationship with so that they continue to follow you, pay attention to your offerings, and champion your business.

Developing your brand persona, then, is not too different from developing a character for a novel. However, here you are not developing an entirely new character, but instead, you are looking for the aspects of your personality that you want to highlight for your brand, so that you can have a clear character to present to your target audience. You will be looking at how you can develop your voice, tone, look, personality, story, and more so that it is clear with whom you are sharing your audience.

As you develop your character, keep in mind that you want to develop a character that is both authentic and that fits with your target niche. You do not want to develop a persona that is too different from who you truly are, as it will feel like you are always acting. Your audience will likely see the discrepancies between who you show up and who you claim to be. By homing in on your authentic personality and choosing to amplify that part of your personality, you can ensure that you are connecting with your audience in an authentic way. This way, you can maintain your persona and develop it strongly and profoundly.

Who Are You and Why Are You Different?

The first thing you need to identify when developing your brand persona is who you are and why you are different from everyone else in your niche. Consider this as the foundation for the persona that you will create, as you want to really get into the core of who you are and how you plan to show up for your audience. Here, you want to consider both how you want to show up and how your audience needs you to show up to develop a personality that is relevant to you while also developing one that your audience is likely to respond to. This way, you can develop a personality that feels fun and enjoyable to partake in, and that is well received by the people who are going to be responsible for helping you generate profits in your business!

You want to start the process of developing your persona by getting into the meat of who you are. The best way to do this is to identify some keywords that highlight your personality, your core values, and what your mission is in the world. These three areas of who you are will help give you some insight as to how you show up, what you like to share with the world, and what you can offer to your audience in terms of a personality for them to relate with. The chances are that you have many core values, a few different life goals, and several aspects of your personality that stands out to you. If this is the case, you can identify your overall personality and all of your values and goals that relate to your industry and the brand you are building. If you need to narrow it down even further, you can also narrow down which elements of your personality are going to suit your brand the best, so that you are really clear on what personality needs to be amplified for your audience.

Once you have gotten into the meat of who you are, you can begin to identify what it is about you that is going to resonate most with your audience. They are most likely looking for something fairly consistent in the industry you are in, so many of your values, goals, and personality traits will overlap with people who are already in your chosen industry. That is totally fine, and to be expected. In fact, if you were *too* different, you may not fit very well into the industry so do not be afraid to be a part of the pack in terms of having a similar persona to those around you.

Now that you have identified the core of who you are and the main elements of what makes you who you are, you can start focusing on where your uniqueness is. At your core, you are likely to be similar to your competition, but there needs to be more about you that helps set you apart from everyone else who is already out there, doing the same thing. Suppose you look at those who have climbed to the top of their industries. In that case, it is always because they had something different about them that was unique to their brand experience. Those who are not climbing faster are often trying too hard to fit into the industry, so they find themselves being overshadowed by the many others who show up with the same manufactured or plain personality that fails to stand out amongst the crowd.

Think about it: if you scroll through Instagram's Style (Discovery tab), are you more likely to look at the 800 photos that all look the same, or are your eyes going to immediately spot the one or two that are different from the rest? The chances are that your eyes will look for the differences. This is because those who are different or unique stand out to us and catch our eye. They are not like everyone else; they have something that helps set them apart from the crowd, so rather than having our eyes glaze over we begin to pay attention to them. For you to get yourself out there, you need to be that one person who is doing things differently so that people pay attention to you.

Being unique in online space comes in two layers: your appearance and your personality. Since the social media world is highly based on visual aesthetics, you need to have an appearance that is different from everyone else's if you are going to find a way to stand apart from the crowd and develop your uniqueness online. You can develop a unique look by finding one or two aesthetics that you like and that are relevant to your brand, but not widely used in your industry and others use those as your features. For example, Amanda Frances, a self-made millionaire and business coach, highlights cash and the colors white, gold, and pink as her primary colors. Most people from her audience can identify her by these two things. These two aesthetics help her stand out from the rest of the business coaches in the online space. Another great example is Kiki Davies from Pursuing Pretty, which is a popular fashion blogging website. Kiki is well known for her bright and lively colors and the outdoor urban-esque photoshoots that she does to highlight her favorite outfits.

Creating a very specific image for your brand makes it easier for your audience to identify you when they see you online. Those who are new to your page can immediately tell whether or not they enjoy your aesthetic, and those who have followed you for a while will be able to pick you apart from others based on your aesthetic. Furthermore, using consistent imagery like this for your audience can create a great sense of consistency that results in your audience thinking of you when they see things in their day-to-day life that remind them of you. For example, suppose you love rainbows and you regularly post pictures of rainbows or rainbow colors. In that case, your loyal audience members will begin to associate you with rainbows. Therefore, every time they see a rainbow, they will think about you, and they will be inspired to see what you are up to or catch up with you in the online space.

As you choose your two things, make sure that they will relate to your audience in one way or another so your aesthetic matches that which your audience would be looking for. So, if your audience is a professional one, using kittens as part of your aesthetic will probably not help find whom you are looking for. You need to pick an aesthetic that is going to appeal to your audience, while remaining both authentic to you and standing apart from the rest of the crowd. If you cannot think of two things quickly, consider checking out your competition and seeing what they are doing to gain some inspiration for how you can set yourself apart. Refrain from allowing yourself to directly copy someone else, as this will cause you to lose your authenticity and will result in you being seen as a copycat. Instead, use their uniqueness as inspiration to find your own thing so that you can begin developing a specific image for yourself that is unique to you.

Identifying Your Voice

In addition to identifying what you want to look like for your audience, you also need to identify how you want to sound, or what you want to be saying to your audience. The tone you share with your audience can play a huge role in connecting with the people you are talking to, as can the language. By identifying the right tone and vocabulary to use, you can ensure that you are connecting with your audience in a way that they relate to and receive.

There are two ways that you can identify a voice for your brand: first by identifying what voice you already have, and second by identifying what the most effective voice in your industry is. You will combine these two voices to generate a voice that is authentic to you while still effectively reaching your target audience.

CHAPTER 8:

Creating an Online Presence

ffiliate marketing is all about creating an effective online presence. Besides great content, using the right platform can help you build the type of interaction you need to engage users. In contrast, the wrong approach to building your online presence can have detrimental consequences. This is why you need to consider all of the options available to you to make the best decision.

Most affiliate marketers focus their efforts solely on social media. And while social media is certainly effective, there is only so much you can do with it. Eventually, social media will run its course. Thus, you need to have a presence across various media. That will allow you to heighten your reach. Moreover, you'll be able to reach your target market more effectively.

We are going to be looking at the various platforms that you can explore. We'll also discuss which ones fit better given the type of content present. In the end, the choice of a platform must consider the type of users you are looking to engage in. As you will see, you can make your presence felt across a myriad of media. Consequently, there is no need to focus solely on social media.

Do take the time to ponder the best outlet to present your content. Please try to resist the temptation to copy what everyone else is doing. Keep in mind that what works for some doesn't necessarily work for others. You need to develop your style and presence. As a result, leveraging platforms to your advantage is a must.

Becoming A Blogger

Creating a blog is one of the first stops for affiliate marketers. By definition, blogs are text-heavy. This means that you can present a great deal of information to your followers. As such, a blog is a great way of providing consistent and highly detailed information.

Blogs are very useful especially since social media limits the amount of text you can present. Twitter only allows you 144 characters. Instagram isn't built for text. As for Facebook, overly long posts generally go unnoticed. Consequently, a blog makes sense if you are planning on providing copious amounts of information. Plus, you can organize information in a digestible manner. This not only facilitates understanding, but it also allows users to reference your material.

Travelers use blogs to chronicle their journeys. For instance, they use blogs to know destinations, hotels, and airlines and describe their experiences. Also, subject matter experts use blogs to provide users with detailed information. Virtually any professional can exploit a blog to their benefit. A blog can become a repository for reference information.

Platforms such as WordPress enable creators to embed various types of content. For instance, YouTube videos can fit in nicely. Additionally, social media sites can easily redirect traffic from a post to the blog. This strategy is often used. A social media post serves to entice users to visit the blog. There, they can find all the details on the topic.

Suppose you are considering product reviews, offering expert advice, providing step-by-step instructions, or chronicling some kind of journey. In that case, a blog is a great place to have as your starting point. From there, users can branch out to other platforms. In particular, your blog should contain links to all of your affiliate pages. Do not neglect to include as many links as possible.

Mailing Lists

Nowadays, most marketers neglect mailing lists. Often, they feel that mailing lists are outdated. However, they can be a great source of engagement especially if you can provide valuable content. Mailing lists can provide you with periodic contact with your users.

Due to regulations, you need to get users to sign up for your mailing list. To get users to sign up willingly, you need to provide them with content they can use. This generally comes in the form of a regular newsletter. Depending on your product, your newsletter can be daily, weekly, or monthly. Once a user signs up, they get your content in their inbox. This content should compel them to visit any of your platforms. From there, they can hit any of your affiliate links. In some cases, marketers openly suggest users visit their affiliates straight from their inbox.

Building mailing lists takes time. It usually implies building a strong following across various platforms. For instance, you can produce content for YouTube and ask viewers to sign up for your mailing list. The same can be done on social media. From a social media post, users can be redirected to your sign-up page.

The only problem with mailing lists is spamming. If you send out content too frequently, you may end up turning off your users. So, it's best to email less frequently than you'd like. Here are some examples to consider:

- If you deal with products that folks regularly consume (cosmetics, food and drink, clothes, shoes, entertainment) you can try emailing daily.
- News outlets and publishers often email daily (once a day only)
- Luxury goods email weekly or twice a month.
- Niche products (those that have a very specific market) email less frequently
- Entertainers email very frequently (music and movie streaming sites, for instance)

Based on these guidelines, you can assess where you stand. Please bear in mind that if your product has a high turnover, then you might consider upping the frequency of your contact. The last thing you want to do is tire your users. So, it's best to start slow and ramp up your contact rather than having to scale back.

Social Media

Just about every marketer starts with social media. Logic dictates that social media should be the starting point for any successful digital marketing endeavor. However, those that swear by social media learn that the internet is a vast expanse. As such, limiting yourself to social media is very narrow-minded.

The purpose of social media is to create engagement. This type of engagement should compel your users to follow you, leading to your users hitting those affiliate links. Often, this might mean hitting the links straight from your social media pages or visiting your blog.

Social media is also great if you are looking to promote other platforms. This type of cross-selling is great because it allows you to keep your users hopping from one place to another. This is important because practically all users have some kind of presence across various platforms. So, you might find they spend time on YouTube, Facebook, and Twitter. Thus, linking your users across various platforms is a great way of keeping engagement up.

So, let's take a look at how you can leverage the various social media platforms out there.

- Facebook

Nowadays, Facebook is seen as a classic. It's a staple of social media. However, it is no longer the hottest place to be. Facebook is still quite popular with the older crowd. Please bear in mind that Facebook was the only show in town for a while. Therefore, a vast number of users became accustomed to Facebook. As more platforms emerged (such as Snapchat or Instagram), younger users preferred these to Facebook.

Facebook is a great platform when you have a balanced approach between text and image. If your marketing endeavors target older audiences, and you present a text-image combo, then Facebook is a good place to start. However, avoid long texts as much as possible. Extremely long texts (anything beyond 150 words) will not compel users to read them. The most successful posts use 50 words or less. Additionally, Facebook makes a great trampoline. From here, you can get users to visit your Instagram, YouTube, Snapchat, or Twitter sites. Plus, you can use it to redirect users to affiliate links, blogs, or online shops.

- Instagram

Instagram is built on imagery. This means that images say it all. This is why fashion brands exploit Instagram. Influencers also make a living out of it. Suppose you are looking to promote anything in the world of fashion, lifestyle, travel, or experiences. In that case, Instagram is the place to be. It's also the place to be when looking to access a younger demographic.

Using short video clips is also a very useful technique on Instagram. Short clips can be used to send a message or present a call to action. Instagram can also be used to redirect users to affiliate links. However, it doesn't work quite as well as a trampoline. So, don't be afraid to ask users to visit your affiliate links rather than your blog or website.

- TikTok

TikTok is a relative newcomer to the scene. However, its popularity has been meteoric. It is used by influencers that like to maintain a consistent presence in the minds of their followers. You can use this platform if you need an alternative to Instagram. Moreover, it's a hit with teenagers. Hence, if your products are directed at teenagers, TikTok is the place to be.

To succeed on this platform, you ought to show your products in action. Any product works as long as you can produce a short clip depicting your product in action. However, try to avoid much of the silliness that you see on this platform. You want to make sure that your users keep their eyes on the ball the whole time.

- Twitter

Twitter is text-heavy. This is a great platform for those seeking to maintain a great deal of contact with their followers. Publishers, news media, and highly influential individuals use Twitter frequently. Given the restrictive nature of 144 characters, you need to be precise in what you say. As such, Twitter can be a great complement to other social media sites. You can leverage Twitter as a means of staying on top of the game. If you are providing content that your users need to know right away, Twitter is the place to be. Everything from celebrity gossip to the latest product releases is a fair game on Twitter. Additionally, Twitter can be a great alternative to mailing lists.

- Reddit and Quora

These sites don't get as much attention as they should. These sites are text intensive. So, they are great for people seeking very specific information. You can build a presence here especially if you are an expert in your field. You might find it interesting to see people seeking your advice. That is why using threads on these sites can provide you with the opportunity to redirect users to your blog, website, or YouTube. However, sending them to social media may defeat the purpose of a purely text-based interaction.

Video Streaming

YouTube is the king of video streaming. Virtually anyone who's anyone needs a YouTube channel. Since YouTube is imminently visual, it is a great platform for anyone looking to do product reviews and demos. It's also great for anyone looking to provide exposure to brands.

However, YouTube is also used by podcasters. You should not overlook this alternative. For those types of products that allow for deep discussion, creating YouTube-based podcasts makes sense. For instance, experts, commentators, and analysts use YouTube as a means of providing in-depth information. YouTube can also provide a visual alternative to blogging. Hence, the concept of a vlog can go hand in hand with a regular blog.

CHAPTER 9:

Social Media Tools

T hese tools can help you keep track of consumers' demographics, make it simpler when messages or videos are posted, and streamline your experience with social media.

Choosing the Best Social Media Platform for Your Job in Marketing

We will look at different useful options for your marketing needs for social networking sites. To decide what is successful, you can look at several points relating to the various social media sites. Of course, with all the social networking platforms we mention here, you can still collaborate with as many as you want to make yourself available. However, that doesn't mean that everyone is reasonable for your needs, let alone easy to use. Based on how it targets and how it is structured, each social networking platform is different. Each site on social media is unique. In preparing your social media strategy, choose carefully. It is best to have several social networking platforms since it gives you the chance to do more. Centered on what you can deal with, we will look at individual social networking sites.

Google Analytics

Suppose you have a blog or a website to which you link your social media account. In that case, you will likely have Google Analytics available already. If it isn't available, then you can update it on your website or blog immediately.

In November 2005, this software was introduced. It's free to use, and it's a lot better than a messy visitor counter. Google Analytics helps you see how many organic (not repeat) visitors you received, where they came from, how long they were on your website, and what particular pages they were viewing.

In 2011, it was dramatically modified to include a personalized dashboard, real-time data, and an influential built-in social media analytics report. Suppose you don't monitor the number of visitors to your blog. How can you say it makes a difference to your social media presence? Ideally, you want to install this before you begin your social media activities to make sure that there is a difference in visitors' numbers when you start your social media marketing.

Analytics from the Internet

In a quantitative framework, social media analytics help frame the interactions. For the origins of the exchange, the influencer metrics do the same. Between these, you have the basis for evaluating progress according to your set's business goals and the KPIs you have developed (Key Performance Indicators). The next step is to connect these to your business, starting with its presence online.

Performance of Websites

The output of your website or online applications is primarily involved in web analytics. What is typically meant by success is how well your website turns visitors into clients. These people help your cause via contributors or enlisted volunteers, or some similar transformation into your purchasing or acquisition funnel that takes them all the way. There are a variety of testing points provided by web analytics.

Understanding the individual metrics and then going past them is the secret to getting the best out of your web analytics program. Too many businesses track the basics, bounce rate; time spent, page views, but then fail to step past these simple counts and into what drives them and why they matter in actual analytics.

Analytics for Market

Social media's market application is, or should be, guided by its relation to business. The ties between social media analytics and web analytics culminate in a systematic testing method to identify the relationships (correlation) that drive outcomes and then extract the leading practices (causation) that can be repeated to develop your company. These approaches can initially be restricted to marketing.

The case for social media marketing initiatives was to design and create new outreach points. Places where individuals within the company could engage on behalf of the brand for clients, social networks are a marketing medium. The next segment takes the strategies useful in marketing and extends them to the enterprise as a whole, where the emphasis turns to business analytics. In particular, there is a measurable relation to business in the case of social media and the Social Web, represented by a result against a collection of defined business goals. The end goal needs to be that degree of understanding, and you need to be relentless about getting there.

Bit.ly

You may think it's strange to have a link shortening service, but it's a huge benefit to shorten links. Historically, since there was a character limit of 140 characters, this was used by social media marketers who were marketing on Twitter. It would be a giant waste of space to use a complete URL. Twitter has solved this problem by making their own shortened link for their site, so why use it?

Tracking is the key. Not only can most URL shortening services shorten your links, but they will give you monitoring services and analytics. You can monitor social networks from a single dashboard when you use the same URL shortened for your social network links, and see how many clicks you have received.

Analytics is the beauty of this particular shortening service. For you, Bit.ly has an incredible amount of knowledge. They tell you how many times a link has been clicked in a tweet or what network the user has been using. You can customize the look of your short URL by inserting a custom URL shortened if you'd like to be posh. So instead of using bit.ly at the start of the URL, yours will be used!

Buffer

Buffer helps you to upload or share all the sites on which you are on the social network. This tool varies from most traditional social media management systems because it is for updates to be scheduled. The bonus is, when your followers and supporters are most likely to be there, you can post on Facebook or Twitter. Once you're at home relaxing, your followers might use Twitter or Facebook in the evening. Still, Buffer will post automatically at the times you want during the week. It helps you upload profiles, pages, groups, profiles, LinkedIn pages, Instagram, and Google+ pages to Facebook and Twitter. Whenever you add a post to this service, you pick the network or networks to which you want it to go. It is added to the system's queue—buffer posts in the row and the same for every other network. You like it when it's time for you to post next to your Facebook profile. If you're going to publish immediately, then you can do so. You don't have to wait in a queue. Just using one button in your browser, sharing your articles is simple to do. If you find an item that you know is important to your LinkedIn followers and Twitter followers, click the Buffer button in your browser, add the link and title to those social media networks, and instantly send it or add it to the queue. There is also software you can use for Buffer on your mobile devices so that you can do this anywhere you have an internet connection!

DoShare

It's a shame that Buffer doesn't allow your Google+ profiles to be shared, but DoShare allows you to do it. How does a small business have the time to invest in them, with so many social networks out there? Using social media management software, such as Buffer, which allows you to share on Facebook, Twitter quickly, and LinkedIn is the only way. You have to utilize DoShare for Google+. Many social networking apps do not integrate with Google+ because Google has not released an API for their Google+ profiles.

DoShare lets you post an extension to your Google+ profile and pages that you can use in your Google Chrome browser. As you can plan posts during the week, it functions in a similar way to Buffer. The only difference is that you need to keep your tab open when you want the most update. If there is a server or a computer in your company, this should not be a problem.

Feedly

One of the most imperative lessons for small companies is not to make it all about the business when it comes to using a social media network. If you're sharing posts about yourself, then a social network platform's argument is missing. It's about sharing content with others, too. If you invest in them, people are more likely to invest in you, particularly if you're sharing content they've shared. How do you find and keep an eye on their content, however? Create a list of websites and blogs that you want to keep abreast of. Some websites will create excellent content that you can share, and that is interesting.

When you've got more than five or ten, it can be challenging to keep up with them all at once. That's where readers of the feed come in. Feedreader applications take the RSS feeds from the websites and blogs that you want to keep an eye on and list them in an easily accessible manner for you. Feedly is an excellent app that you can use on your mobile device or in your browser. You can save articles later or post them immediately using Buffer or directly on the social media network you want to post them. It enables you to conveniently share all of your social media networks during the week, in addition to keeping up with the latest news.

MailChimp

It is a marketing service and email newsletter that has an established track record. MailChimp sends out over four billion emails per month and takes care of all the problems that can arise from sending emails to customers. Social media is crucial for your company, but sometimes it takes an email to get them there. To sign up for Facebook and Twitter likes and comments, you need a valid email address, and you have push notifications sent to your telephone to warn you when someone has tagged you or updated their Facebook newsfeed. Thus, email is still essential. Many small companies must build up a database of email contacts. It helps you to learn more about future clients and your existing ones. MailChimp makes this simple, and you can add more detail, such as demographics, over time, which helps marketing campaigns for social media.

It isn't effortless to make sure the website runs well in modern browsers. The days are gone when the only thing you had to think about was working with Internet Explorer. Now, Google Chrome, Opera, Firefox, Safari, and several Internet Explorers are there to work with. There are also smartphone applications on top of that. MailChimp had spent more than ten years ensuring that email newsletters hit the inboxes of customers looking as stunning as they did when you sent them. They have comprehensive analytics, so when they open your email or click through to a website connection, you can track recipients. Although many of these features are free, you have to upgrade if you want more from MailChimp (wishing to submit to more than 2,000 subscribers). Their rates are fair, however.

CHAPTER 10:

Tips and Suggestions for Your Business to be More Online

S ocial networking can be an excellent resource for any brand or company to keep its customers happy. When you have satisfied customers, you will cultivate the company's loyalty and the devotees of your life.

Tweeting Customer Service

Delivering high-quality customer service is a sure-fire way to ensure customer loyalty. They are more likely to buy from a company when they know that any complaints or problems will be dealt with immediately. Usually, customer service inquiries are handled via phone, email, or live chat support. For some instances, however, it is much easier to provide help and pay attention to the needs of users on social media.

Twitter is one of the sites that are useful for addressing customer service problems. Suppose you use social media to offer and handle customer service. In that case, it tells other consumers that the company and brand value their products and walk the extra mile to serve their customers.

Getting to Know Your Brand

Social media channels have always been a perfect place to highlight the personality of your brand. With social media, you can talk directly to your users and consumers and let them know your brand better. Building a relationship with users interprets into brand constancy and generates possible customers.

Creating a Story About Your Brand

In reality, social media is primarily visual, making it laidback for marketers to make stories around their goods and themselves.

Principally for ecommerce products, marketing is not just about promoting a product or accent its services, and it's about creating a lifestyle or a philosophy that defines the products you're selling. You are using social media to share a lifestyle that is designed around your company and make it so that people want to be part of your brand.

Establishing Brand Heroes

Consumers want to shop with brands they can trust. Pulling back the curtain and exposing the people who work behind the scenes is a perfect way to create trust with your customers. If you highlight any of your company's champions, it makes your brand sound less like a corporate agency and more like a friend. With 1.2 million and 45,500 followers on Twitter and Instagram, it shows how critical the brand's personality is.

Engaging Your Customers

And now that you've built up your brand's reputation, it's time to connect with them on a substantive level. Of course, when you think about participation, you're going to have to talk about the material.

Putting a Spotlight on Them

One of the best ways to engage your users and consumers is to support and promote the content they have built on your website. More frequently than not, the customers are already focused on creating their individual social media presence — captivating a selfie with their original pair of shoes or dresses. When you show the content, they've created on your website, it makes your users feel like they're respected by your company.

Creating Value-Added Content

Sharing user content is fine, but it's not enough. You do need to create and share your own high-quality, useful, or entertaining content. Once you have both interesting and useful content, you give your customers a reason to keep coming back to your site and stay there, rather than just shopping around. Get them to live long enough and they're going to end up shopping anyway.

Of course, the other big advantage of having quality content is that it will boost your organic visibility in search engine rankings. Google likes content that addresses people's issues and places the content on social media to make sure that a lot of users use it.

Exploring Digital Media

There are a lot of advertisement incentives in social media. Since most of your potential customers are on social media, it is worth considering investing in social media ads as part of your social strategy.

The Power of Influencers

Influencers are the taste-makers of the social media landscape. A lot of people follow them as they give insight into items that are trendy, fashionable, or interesting. Using social media influencers is a great way to bring your brand to a whole new audience.

Partnering with the right social media influencer that applies to your company will help make your brand more aware of it. Plus, most influencers tend to have many followers willing and able to buy something they see being used or worn.

Suppose you're an organization that already has good aesthetics and a great persona. In that case, you can use that to your benefit and set up a dedicated social media follow-up. Using social media, you can use this tool to develop your brand loyalty, share your brand's story and, most importantly, better meet your customers' needs. All of these will help the company and brand grow to a different level.

10 Rules for Using Social Media to Grow Your Company

Whether you're a social butterfly or apprehensive when it comes to vociferously engaging with others in a public space, there are certain underlying guidelines to be followed when it comes to social networking. Not only will this assist you to develop your social media skills by increasing your base of fans and followers, but it will also allow you to leverage the power you create to gradually grow and extend the scope of your company in every industry or niche.

1. You know your market.

The first rule to grow your business through the power of social media is to know your audience. The clearer you are regarding your demographic goals, the more you will be able to cater to your customers. The less you learn about your demographic target, the less likely you will achieve via social media.

2. Develop a plan for this.

Creating a famous social media profile takes a job. But it also needs to be planned. You need to build a rock-solid plan to achieve every goal. Build your strategy for how you want to get from Point A to Point B. Are you going to use ads? Influents? Users of power? Which kind of material are you going to post? When are you going to publish it? And so on.

3. Depend on content over the number of messages.

The aim is not to bomb post users. It's not about size, it's about the consistency of the messages. Ensure that the posts are tailored to your audience and that each of them conveys a significant message or unique presentation of something specific to that group will help you gain the most attention while also attracting more followers.

4. Create a real interest.

Social media is all about value development. What kind of interest do your posts bring? Are they inspiring or educational in any way? They're helping to inspire people out there to follow a similar lifestyle.

5. Join our high-profile accounts.

All of the Instagram influencers I've talked to have begun by following other high-profile accounts. This made their first sources of recognition for them. It also helped them assess what was effective for those already at the top of their game.

6. Post and like a lot of times.

Anyone serious about using social media to expand their company needs to realize what they have to offer before they do. Genuinely appreciate, comment, and share the posts of others every single day, building relationships with people over time. It's not going to happen overnight. If you don't owe people the time of day, you can't ask them to do the same thing for you.

7. Increase the strength of other influencers.

Influencers and power users will open a door to the attention of the masses. If you have the right profile form that is in alignment with the influencer's follower base, you may just get the right type of followers yourself. Many companies and startups are using this method to help them hit early. If you have a budget, you may want to consider this and ensure that you have attractive material on your profile.

8. Network, network, network, network.

Puia Shamsossadati, the founder of @thisisamans.world, who has accumulated more than 2 million followers, spent most of his time networking with others. He introduced a business called Golden Concept exclusively through Instagram without investing a dime on conventional ads. The company that makes high-end iPhone covers achieved mass appeal when Shamsossadati partnered with some of the most famous Instagram influencers by sending them courtesy phones, realizing that they would show up in their feed them to support their business at virtually no cost.

9. Don't always encourage it.

It's not just a matter of support. If you want to use social media and networks to make your business expand, you need to spend a lot of time providing value. If it's positive worth, motivational worth, or entertainment worth, do not continuously attempt to trade it to people at every turn and turn, or you might put them off.

10. Make it convenient for people to buy it.

Focus on mobile if you're going to conquer social media. Build a connection to your profile, ensure that your site has a well responsive proposal, and style it as easy-to-buy. Certify that the purchasing process is optimized for portable devices so that customers can quickly and conveniently buy whatever you're peddling. The simpler you're going to make things for them to buy, the more likely you're going to be to sell.

Conclusion

How does the future look like? What's going to happen to our businesses?

We can't foresee that with certainty, but we must be prepared.

I hope you found useful ideas and inspiration in this book and I hope you will apply the principles and the techniques you learned to get your business ready for the new era.

Whether people's mobility will be limited in the future, whether everything will be back to normal as we all hope, you need to master two main skills: the ability to sell online and the ability to give your customer a unique experience. You need to become better and better at combining technical skills from the future and interpersonal skills from the past.

Marketing businesses have never been this easy with the advent of the Internet. Businesspersons not only find it convenient to market their brands over the Internet, but they also find it affordable. YouTube is one of the leading social media pages out there. With millions of people accessing it on a daily basis, it means that it stands as a great platform to market your brand. Just like Facebook, people expect to communicate with brands in a natural way. Therefore, the marketing strategies that you employ will make a difference in your campaign. Unique marketing strategies that you use will definitely make you a loveable brand among your audience.

One of the most important considerations that should be remembered is the fact that the message is very important. What you tell your audience about your product or service will give them an overall picture of your brand. Crafting the right message will, therefore, have a positive impact on your audience. As had been recommended, you need to keep it short. Your message should also be clear. If your audience cannot figure out exactly what you are selling, then you need to redraft your message again.

Social media is the singular, most powerful tool in reaching out to a large number of people. If you do not make it a part of your marketing strategy, especially if you are a small business venture, then you will find yourself facing a huge loss in the digital world of today, where everything runs on hashtags and comments.

You now know what emotions you need to trigger in your customers so they will come back. You learned how to hustle your way into customer acquisition with free techniques that will allow you to expand your network. You may be thinking already about how to simplify your communication and restructure your offer. You know how to launch your campaigns online and what channel to choose. You know how to spy on your competitors, how to portray your business online, and tweak your cover to increase your success.

You learned how organic reach works and how to hack your growth on social media, how to create content, plan it and organize it in a short period of time, and you learned the secret of an outstanding website that sells.

Take a pen and paper and write down your goals and ideas.

Start working on it today. Don't wait.

Take a small step every day and you will achieve your goals faster than you think.

CPSIA information can be obtained
at www.ICGtesting.com
Printed in the USA
BVHW062331010321
601388BV00009B/1188